THE GLAZIER'S CHOICE

T0160155

THE GLAZIER'S CHOICE

Charles Wilkinson

EYEWEAR PUBLISHING

First published in 2019
by Eyewear Publishing Ltd
Suite 333, 19-21 Crawford Street
Marylebone, London W1H 1PJ
United Kingdom

Cover design and typeset by Edwin Smet
Printed in England by TJ International Ltd, Padstow, Cornwall

All rights reserved
© 2019 Charles Wilkinson

The right of Charles Wilkinson to be identified as author of
this work has been asserted in accordance with section 77
of the Copyright, Designs and Patents Act 1988
ISBN 978-1-912477-85-2

MIX
Paper from
responsible sources
FSC® C013056

WWW.EYEWEARPUBLISHING.COM

For Alistair Davies

Charles Wilkinson's work includes *The Snowman and Other Poems* (Iron Press, 1987) and *The Pain Tree and Other Stories* (London Magazine Editions, 2000). His poems have appeared in *Poetry Wales, Poetry Salzburg* (Austria), *Shearsman, The Reader, New Walk, Magma, Under the Radar, Tears in the Fence, Scintilla, Envoi, Orbis, Stand, The Warwick Review, Snow lit rev, Gargoyle* (USA) and other journals. A pamphlet, *Ag & Au*, came out from Flarestack Poets in 2013. *A Twist in the Eye*, his collection of weird fiction and strange tales, was published by Egaeus Press in 2016. *Splendid in Ash*, from the same publisher, came out in 2018. He lives in Powys, Wales.

TABLE OF CONTENTS

THE HIDEAWAY SLEEP

THE GLAZIER'S CHOICE

THE WORDS MOVING AWAY

It as if you could die without a self, your lost properties
dispersed: that bag of kindness resting on a shelf, this
holdall grief you kept your sorrows in bereft on some
forgotten station, the folder where your paper dreams
were filed, damp and yellow in the skip.

        Fields delete themselves
on journeys, leaving an after-image of greenness;
the fences that kept you off the grass go by.

  The luggage was lost an hour before: your fist
clenched where the handle vanished; an empty space
about your feet. The roving eye saw figures fleeing
into air; a lure of distant colour changed shade as you
approached; hope stalked out into the street. Yet
wasn't there a tote of joy that made the trip?

         Here's the halt,
no waiting room, only a sign, the gate swinging in
the almost silence. Your fingers searching every
pocket for something unnamed but missed.

          Evening.
The faint beat of a far-off music, the high notes heard
somewhere else. A smooth taut sky's deepening blue
holds only the promise of stars, the shine of a drumhead
moon.

  Your walk from an unmanned station: lit carriages
seen between the trees, the collected speed that moves
through counties, past lakes and pines, hills and castles.

      A sign to an unknown village.
And now the book you left on the train hurrying towards
darkness, carrying its ending to the last stop on the line.

VOID POST

Mornings, we wake askew in the world:
the day's been put through the wrong box
or thrown over the hedge to lighten the bag.
Our hopes are away with the birds, posted
with their wings fixed: the stamped chevrons
on a flight that's unlocated; clouds deliver rain
to a distant address.
                    Now this rook flying
diminishes, switching from comma to stop.
The sentence is hidden far underground
or forwarded to the deep side of the sky:
a space that is undisturbed, where the letter
is open and held in the hand.
               Here is now's almost nothing, except
believing, some days, in the sealed instructions
that wait on a table in a cool dark hall, leading
to the room where love allows high singing
& the call of light.
             The telephone rings, unheard. Words,
meant for us, collect in the silence of an empty house.

LOOKING IN

From the street, you can see right through the house
and into the garden. Skipping the lives and furniture
gives a glimpse of brown leaf buffed to a leather gleam
by double glaze, a paler gloss of sky; the light's
furred in one frame.

You will have to imagine the lawn,
where an orange ball, radiant in the grass, is a globe
of flame imported from a day in Spain – and that child's
swing, suspended in perpetual play.

In the drive these two cars,
parked side by silk-like side, lead on to thoughts
of later warmth within the walls: the windows filling
with the lamp's oloroso glow; his hand laid on
hers, gentle as clover; the burnished wood on which
two glasses touch where the gold of wine is steeped
in the fireside's scarlet; and, so soft beneath their feet,
the new and dustless carpet.

Outside, you are looking in as the sky
changes and cloud lays a wash of shadow. Knowing
the rain will stop here with you, and this grey light is
yours for ever, will not stop you staring long, as if
reflecting on a land for all the bright occasions, when
in no time sunfall lives – and where you will never stand.

THE GLAZIER'S CHOICE

a sky cloud cobble:
hard unmoving grey,
yet the wind rounds a
corner far below

★

through the car window
trees so tall and ancient —
and I am so small —
they were born in me

★

from my cot I see
stars painted on the
ceiling — no need for
a candle tonight

★

in memory there is
no dawn mist before
the last black kiss
returns us to night

★

which day was the first
no question except
how to configure
each frame of weather

★

winter trees white sky
my hand is on the gate:
antler of blue veins
dark branch thinning snow

★

late summer swifts far
above the garden;
no sound, apart from
the white page turning

★

patch of light on glass
is trapping the room
in the window: dark
bars framing flowers

★

early words are names
of the black cars born
from city suburbs:
hiss-swish through the rain

★

the night light burns low
last thought before sleep:
warplanes that rest on
the floor fly at dawn

★

boy in black and white
stands by the bird bath:
remembered colours
grey blue touch of stone

★

the glazier's choice:
arrange the panes of
memory until
each is turned to light

NO LONGER THE ONLY

I

That was the time you first saw frost

The morning the garden cried star salt

Upstairs for weeks and her door closed

Summer and winter the same

Though blue was a different heat

The hand came down from the ceiling

No chair now you can walk to the park

The grey hair – was it in clouds?

This stranger's voice has come to stay

Your silence knows its place

Some pain, some great event

What has come adds to our shadows

The road was covered in rocks

You have a sister, they say

Their faces look down from the light

II

The new men wear orange

Their night's in a bucket, stirred

The smell comes stinging from the earth

They buried the road in black

She is so small covered by snow

You slam the door in her face

What tars the hands stays

They came and they rolled it flat

You hold her tight, not even a little fall

In sunlight, you stick to the street

This inside tree's white-webbed

This gift, which was yours, is given to her

These cars, these lorries, this crying

You walk differently, holding her hand

Next summer's flowers not all for you

RULE

First thorny words
Follow the spike
Of shadow and
Then the slanting
Line sharpening
From something like
Soft grey cloud to
A charcoal slash
As it falls on
The whiteness of
What will become
And is straightened,
Till matching the
Horizon which
Marks the northern
Limits of what
Is possible,
It tells us that
We must create
In the narrows
That lie so straight
Between the thin
Red rails that lead
Downwards to the
Last line of grey,
Leaving nothing
In the margin,
No word aslant,
So what we have
Done is all that
We could have done
Till the very last
Day and will more
Than justify.

BOARDING THE DARK

first night away   alone with the others
light snapped off   naked bulb's afterburn
& the sheets black   stone slide touch
so faint the edge lost   the bed fathom floating
a foot down space   not finding wood
dark's replacing world   you are all thought
one star exploring   the occupation of night
though now this breath   sending out shadows
as if one shade   lighter than air
and here's a patch   moss-hover on the wall
& this soft bar of grey   suspended gives back space
its every forward move   is furred retreat
shimmering now reforms   the curtains not quite drawn
frail finger on the ceiling   eider's heavy fall
far from slipper dawn   a slow warmth enfolding
the walk through the ride   the trees are leaning closer
they cannot find you here   the boughs are linked by leaf
the quietening of the rain   will teach you not to weep
the path so very clear   the forest's dreaming floor
& each step carries further   along the way to sleep

HIDDEN

Waking too fast & early
turns the dream back
with the bed clothes, leaving
the dust of night-thought
thick on the tongue.

You walk through a flume
of sunlight, the dry motes
hovering in the haze, & back
into the room where darkness
furies at your feet.

Yet thinking, so slow with
words this morning, you
know there's this indivisible day
that shines outside & lets
us live within.

You are: it's the verb
that's the most difficult,
there being no object causes
infinite regret, when all we
have is this glimpse –

a crack in the curtain.
The parts of speech drawn
over the window will not let us
see complete or be certain of
what it is we lack.

This movement is perhaps
a way of trusting. You scarcely

feel the steps that take you down the hall,
the hand that pushes at the door. Forget
the sheets as white as clay:

hear the heart that bids you live
with less than all & confess that now,
awake, the morning is the complement,
& even sleep might never find the gods
hidden in the process.

HALF-HERACLITEAN

shadow of
an angler's rod
splintering
on the stream:
fly-fishing
with a spool
on water that
won't rewind;
no pool where
the current
will hesitate,
only the weir's
flash & scales
in water-cream:
no place to press
pause; just one
thin figure on
a bank, casting
& casting, who's
reflecting on
a river where
nothing's reeled in
from time, as he
waits for a bite,
without bait or hook;
& no catch, forever
in the flow, beneath
his weightless line

THE DEFECTIVE LENS

I have seen
no thin God
or his tall
murderers,
yet I share
a way of
looking with
The Greek:
our stigmata
the wounds of
sight, though
his saviour
has long lines
of blood
for-giving;
I found only
a shadow
with no veins
caught in
the lean grey
sun, walking
away from
the garden,
& saving
no one.

THE TRUE SUN

wishing to walk
down the street
as if you know how
to live here, you see
the sun is behind
the tall buildings,
the road in shadow,
though there is a
glow of gap between
two houses so that
one bridge of light
falls, as if it could
tempt you to cross
to what's open &
giving on the other
side; somehow you
have now forgotten
yourself in the day
& every moment
over place is loss:
the way as you move
you pass it, the one
path over darkness,
without ever stopping
to feel the true sun
touching your face

THE CLEARANCE

The play of these
narrow lanes is
lassoed into
new design
& ringed around
the centre; how
to touch the place
that's gone? The cam-
ber's different now:
you creak over
the space where you
once ran; when all's
re-routed here,
& no tree clings in clay,
there are those last
ghosts behind these
words; the past and
now are back to back;
there's something
here deriving, a
trace of a lost speech,
the voice you once
knew rising to call
you from the street,
the half-remembered
phrases heard with
ear against the thinnest
wall. Now when you
walk you sense it near:
a tap upon the shoulder,
a child's trick that turns
you back the wrong way

but there's no laughter
now — or racing steps:
only the empty
road that looks both
ways, facing what
was — and has no face.

THE TRAIN LIBRARY

— eyes closed and the escalator's
rail-rattle is under the bay;
study in silent area, though
far-off voices in the stacks hush
and turn the page of steam; first
the trolley turns smooth wheels — then
the clatter over points, jolts,
shaking a change of line, Level 3:
its load of Applied Art, Textiles
freighted with Industrial Design;
in mortared books lie crescents, squares
& streets, their truth long imprinted
on the land, though here's the pencil's
scratch — a spire, a dome — of shapes
departing for the world, and these shelves
hold the vanished orders, the dreams
of brick and stone.

              & now blinked back
the passengers' vertical ascent brings
new bindings from first floor fictions
to high trees of family, networked
into branches of the living
& the cut; the top storey, its
aisles of texts: the dates of deaths, &
down to name the new-berthed, trav-
elling to what destinations,
the fares unfixed — all flowering;

yet this place is
            a state dissolved

and built over; in dust's will, re-
signed to loss, these motes inherit,
though hear this announcement: the word
profits on all platforms, & will
embark; attend the darting de-
light, chiaroscuro: tunnel /day,
& keep the flaw that will support:
the story's lie when plied is art.

The first entrance
                    informs: leaflets,
not ready for fall, shine local
attractions of life: there is love's
castle stormed; this garden's recovered
spring. The journey's unreserved
and needs just looking; though this is
where you entered – &
                    will alight

MACON   EVENINGS   GOLD

light is wine glaze
& the glass

memory
of grape

fragrance of
summer six o'clock

terroir
is more than
an inheritance
of shadows

the stain of
vine on earth
this now
of taste
& scent

complexity
is the moment
where
the hand
lifts the weight
of colour
shone through by
eternal sun

TWO GARDENS

For Mary K. Wilkinson

where the walled garden
      holds the shape of light
leaning on stone, there
      a bench, silvered
with age, has been placed
      in the shade from which
are seen the flowers,
      the angel-shiver
of white butterflies,
      the sparrows, painted
chestnut with black flecks
      above pale breasts, and the
sun and shadow mov-
      ing across the stone
walls, warming grey to
      umber, lightening
the mortar until
      the hands of evening
fall. Here is the place
      to remember the
Slain Sheikh, Master of
      Illumination,
al-Suhrawardi,
      executed on
Saladin's orders
      in Aleppo, and the
King's Peacock under
      The Basket, which tells
of a garden drifting
      with water, light and
song, where peacocks flock

across green lawns; the
fragrance of flowers
    carries on the faint breeze
until the King takes
    one of his peacocks
and places it in a
    leather basket in
which there is a small
    seed-hole so it can
be fed. The days fade.
    The peacock comes to
love its leather world
    and forgets the King,
the garden, the water
    and the flowers;
believes that nothing
    lies beyond the warm
basket that it loves.
    Though on some days it
can hear the distant
    sigh of water, smell
the scent of flowers, just catch
    the cries of peacocks,
and is filled with long-
    ing for what it can
no longer understand.
    Yet here felicia,
campanula's pale bells,
    fuschia and aster, yel-
low-eyed, blooming below
    penstemon, its garnet
gleam bright against the green
    of white agapanthus,
are outshone as the slant
    of evening sun flares on

phlox – starfire, harlequin:
        deepest red and purple,
colour glowing against
        the darkening wall: some
paradisial tint
        or this world, radiant –
as if locked in with light.

WATER LAUGHING

around rock, downstream and
      bright in the glitter day;
shaking over stone, licked
      with light; or a fountain's
play, slow grins widening
      across the mirrored arcs;
the cascade's applause, fall-
      ing and rising, fading
into the river, tin
      smile of light, swapping swirl
with the darker ripple,
      rapid over pebble,
and race tumbled before
      running onwards to the
sea's wide mouth; no, it was
      the name of a horse on
which, liking the sound of
      nature laughing, he once
put money. Now reading
      Sheikh al-Suhrawardi's
The Language of the Ants
      he remembers another
translation, one in which
      'laughter' was preferred to
'language', and longs for
      a country where language
is laughing like water.

Note: Suhrawardi (Shibab al-Din Yahya Suhrawardi), a Persian, was executed, on the orders of Saladin (Salah-al-Din) or his nephew, at Aleppo in 1191. He was a Sufi philosopher and the founder of the illuminationist tradition.

ORDER

Every night before you sleep you try to put your life
   in order, though it's not the tidy house, the balanced hours
or friendships kept in bright repair that keep you thinking.
   It's this prayer to a god of sequence who holds each kite
of memory on the line. The wind forgets the shapes
   of elms – and see how this once shining string frays
and turns to cloud. Did you that first time in Spain
   awake in a blue-grey room fragrant with oranges,
a thin white curtain to blur the sun – though light waxed
   upon the window sill? And was this before the wave
that licked the sandcastle off the beach? And when
   were those olive shadows and the scents of evening?
So hard to rank the trembling days and say which colours
   are the liars or name the blue that holds a silver plane
pinned like a brooch to a wayward sky. A trail of white
   flowers fades into water, creates a sadness we never
knew. The lips moving, the fingers telling, as if they
   could make a story out of it. Snap out the light.
In the dark, they'll come sharper – the cherished instants
   clear and true? And to think again of the hand you held,
as if you loved not once but twice! Night. Though
   there's a gleam behind the eye, a tiny figure skating,
a last joy, skilled in the arts of turning, on black ice.

TWITCH

Five months out of the womb
and still bawling; a tea-
spoon of brandy settles
the flail of pudgy hands,
then the palms are fixed and
open, pointing upwards:
some small wicketkeeper
waiting for a catch, sus-
pending the moment up
in the blue-white dazzle.

At three, the rabbit-wrink-
le nose does not concern,
though watching after-rain
sparrows dance, so crazy
in whirrs of wings, sends him
flapping across the lawn,
his fan fingers stirring
air, as if flight could still
the seething flesh, the grins
that itch across the face.

Fourteen – found and lost faith,
crosses uncrosses his
knees; nothing holds his
attention; a tic in the
tiny muscle beneath
the eye, the twitch that breaks
the smile's smooth tide are re-
marked upon. The grey
garden, the blackbirds last
forever – and will not fly.

Once he's forty it is
the pigeon on the off-
ice window sill that gives
colour and gloss; yet will
not stay to watch the zig-
zag market trembling on
his brow, the graphs of gain
and loss. The day stalls when
the system's down in gin-
trapped light. Nobody calls.

Now nearing seventy
brings a wine sipped slowly,
sounds that are no longer
the fingers' impatience,
drumming stock higher, but
the free cries of gulls ris-
ing above the waves, though
the lip will shiver when
the sea fret rolls in, fleec-
ing skyline and ocean.

Alone on the beach – the
sand creases anxiously
with each tide. Too late for
bright castles now, and they
were always washed away.
Yet under the wide sky
he stands, as if watching
the crests for some rare white
miracle, riding in.

THE TEACHER'S CLOTHES DYED IN-SERVICE

tweed green-brown
rugby pitch mud & grass
woven by bodyslide

summer past blazer
cut from a sky half
a yard from nightfall

forty years slipping
between the wiseacres'
cracks – self lost in syllabi

five red pens found
in the old jacket left
in fluffy-dust wardrobe

the stain where the biro
burst in the left inside
pocket during the long lesson

& the ink on the breast
marking the place where
the heart's test went wrong

TO HIS SUCCESSOR

What's personal has been packed
  And parcelled in brown,
Though the brass porcupine,
  Whose quills spiked unwanted
Papers, has been given to a friend;
  The manila shapes, a darker shade,
Will stay as if pasted to the wall
  Where the pictures hung.
Though not greatly lived in,
  This room has seen much use.
The black memory stick
  Will save all that I wish
To forget. To you, who will
  Sit each day at my desk,
I bequeath the view through
  The window: a sky sealed
With grey weather, the birds
That frank the top-right pane,
  Wings waving, as if posted
Straight from purgatory; and
  This room, the antique burns
In the out-tray – memoranda
  Of smokier days – the green
Filing cabinet in the corner,
  Its sickly mouths spewing
Data. The carpet, they say, will be
  Cleaned, but later. Now is the time
To leave, not pausing to pick up
  This sunlight-bill of darkness,
Which lies unopened by the door,
  Square on the shadow's knife.
What's written there will hold

Its shape, and I will pay another
Day, with interest – or more. Here's
   What I took; there's the fire escape.
I wish you good luck with my life.

LEAVING

last day
in the classroom:
low vagrant swallow
foreshadows freedom
flying through the gate.

what will
you take with you
for the rest of summer,
now chairs are stacked &
texts returned to shelves?

look how
final sweepings
raise sundry specks of dust;
these motes are footnotes
of various selves.

draw out
a speckled past,
its pages foxed; though the
library's chained some
links may be unlocked.

keep one
book whose leaves you
turned; say *vade mecum,*
go with me, the best
words I have learned.

SIX MONTHS

Seen for six months from the top flat:
a man dwindling his life on the forecourt
of the half-way house over the road.
He has three T-shirts; the orange one
is favourite. From here his face is narrow,
the line of the lips thin; steel glasses
blank his eyes. He drinks coffee –
or is it tea? Sometimes he stands;
sometimes he sits, askew on the steps,
although he must get up when
visitors arrive. The wind lives
in his scum of sandy hair.
        This autumn
he was seen counting the leaves
before men in yellow jackets came
and put them into bags. A car passing
is always an event. His less is lesser
than our less, we think.
        And yet
tomorrow will bring stark summer,
the police car, shadows of railings
on the stony drive. Two officers
high-holding his arms reminds us
that we have not known him to be
touched before. Although touch, we
will all be told, he has. Is that grin
of sure conviction on his face weak?
Such a wound is a mouth uttering
in the skin, as if pleading to speak.

CHANGE OF USE

The school's been turned
into a retirement home.
Old boys still tell of
the Latin master with
the cleft palate who wore
plus fours, drank between
lessons from a hip flask
and was sacked. Having
used up an allowance of life,
he died by his own hand
in a room with no carpet.

They remember: summers
of whites and strawberries;
reading books in the ha ha;
the high cream of cloud
on immortal blue; cricket –
and cattle on the green land
beyond. The boasts and dares:
jacks and swimming naked
in the pond at midnight.

They think of the clock
in the hall and the marble
staircase that led to the
Headmaster's quarters:
the room and the bed
where he slept in the
scent of sherry breath
with his thin-armed wife.
They recall the stool
over which they bent

to be beaten; the knives
they used to initial trees
and desks. The chalk dust
that caught in the throat;
the ghost stories hidden
in the walnut panelling.

This is the house with
the cast-iron veranda
on which the wisteria snaked,
and here are the windows
that overlooked the lawn
with the rhododendrons
and a great wellingtonia
that almost touched the moon.
This is where they lived and now
pay to die dreaming of a hedgehog
caught in the tennis-net and curled
inside itself, unable to move away
into the world where it awoke
one cold early morning in May.

DOUBLE VISION

…bespangling every bough like stars
— William Blake

The wallpaper was the worst,
stripping and repeating itself
in front of the eye, and later
the bed spinning round before
you vomited after that party
to honour the clever kid's
achievement. 'No wonder
he got a scholarship', you
said, 'he's got two heads.'
              But sober
morning's no joke: the
cap of lead that is your
skull, the thirst that woke
you up at dawn, those pale
stains of self that swim
across your sight.
         Tomorrow must be
a new way of doubling riches
in the world, a day that puts
the glory back into the trees.
            Let's hope for exact
and loving modes of looking,
the tenderness of eye that
treats all objects with lightly
magic care, the fire-fuelled heart
recharging every cell; the stare
that has no pride, but sees
with wide and generous sight,
revising every instant into
lines of gold: the second vision.

THE STORYTELLER

Took us in to start with.
The first line that came dazzling
From the inside pocket;
The cigarette case
Opened so quickly
No one noticed the tarnish.

And in here night after night,
The first round always his.
Three weeks before we spotted him:
Saw how his tales always closed
With a premature snap,
A left hand clawing
The smokeless air
An unstruck match
In the palm of the hand.

And then he was off
To another small hotel,
Another seaside town –
Where sun on the white sand
Confuses the eye
And the sea was bright with possibilities –
Leaving nothing in his empty room
But the windows open,
A girl crying
And the green tie of a club
To which he does not belong
Snaking at the bottom of an open drawer,
Its silver crests glimmering like scales.

THE HUMOUR TREE

(Betula Pendula – Silver Birch)

Though the silver is kept
deep in the wood, summer
it leaks, staining with its
thin milk the dusty bark

or so the boy, who asked
about the birch before
the count of six, is told
along with the story

of the stag's head mounted
on the wall, conker eye
catching the diners' gleam
across the red carpet:

the room at the Raven
where the 'best' people wine
whilst poor cousins sup un–
der the animal's arse

in the restaurant next
door, adjoined in jest
by a mind he cannot
understand; yet the joke

survives the pain, even
the wealth that did not cross
his path, though the man's gone
from brittle ash, along

with trunk, bark and the leaves
of bubble gold; now all
he can hold in the dark
is silver's rooted stump.

THE IRISH SEMIOLOGIST ADVISES THE POET

(County is what they are. J.B.)

Betch yer man's
wearing the dung-coloured jacket
with the salmon pink trousers; he'll
smile at the brogue, though his two
tell yer that he's made his packet:
'Churches give good walking
in a county that's flat, Pat';
and here's the other fella in lovat
green coat and crimson cords:
landowner not farmer is what
the signs say: there's no mud
below the belt round here;
and seasons mix correctly
in the right tweed; no hedge,
no sparrow – and not a weed
in sight; land and sky combine
broadly; the boy's for Harrow.
If there's any shit, you'll not
find it on their shoes, and this
Italian leather on her, so light
it was made for skipping.
They're a couple who leave
sheep dipping to someone else.
Now this brick-faced one, you'd
say, was good for a beer,
but he'll not be drinking in
any bar you're at; there's the wife:
that hat means power – and his life
on Seroxat. Their bard's Sir John.
Your verse is a disgrace. You should
keep your rhymes – and yourself –
in the right place.

FLIGHT ESCAPE

these loops are summer's end,
    knots tightening, as the swifts
        sweep & soar higher. O there is
            no rope that can catch air & every
                year brings back the swifts' unfurling
                    arcs, defying fear; teach us how love
                        lives on the wing, a catching of desire
                    delighting in sky above the spire &
                needing no ring to pair for ever, as in
            our earth-bound rites. Should one swift fall
        take it from the ground with most tender care;
    its home is far, so lift it free for flight, as if
you could be wintering with it, sunlit in Africa.

JACKDAWS

reprieved by sun when
the black-cap becomes purple
& then one cloud pilfering light
turns caddows, college-birds, sea-crows
back to night – with napes
    & half crowns of silver

old glitter-thief: that's
giving you our greed, for
the white eye alone loves easily –
the dance of facets, the shine on
stone set next to the twigs
    in the chimney

little money bird's
a true crow, & legal
to trap; classified, codified,
it's a house's ruin: a mishap wait-
ing to fall, twigs & all,
    down flue to fire

& daws of legend
in the Greek's old tales caught
claws in a fleece or famished saw
how the green figs failed to ripen, like
endings, when the fox taught
    natural law

yet with bills up
real clatterings escape
story, live high with rooks & tell
(we cannot know) in jacks & caws,
quick & slow, their complex calls of
    hidden glory?

VIEW

Regret's the way the tree ramifies
without leaf, the day obscured
in consequence; a moment lies
beneath dense branches rising
from below, & you are so small
alive when from former forests
swindling shadows grow;
recall one white hour as true
or real a single twig; a flower
lies half forgotten in another tense:
the wooden past still builds tall
posts to screen the view. Make
one hole in the fence so looking
through you can watch each
scrap of now passing by – yet
not relumed in old brown light,
but growing green in instant sky.

VACANT POSSESSION

Unhooking the sky
like a curtain,
& later the white clouds:
crumpled sheets in a
suitcase; the moon in
a box, ready to be used
as decoration; the lawn
rolled up into a thin pipe
and tucked under
the arm.
   You think
that you can take
all these props
& leave their shadows
behind? I see you
by a wall of sunlight
bending on one knee,
smiling & empty as you
try to scrape silver from
the bare white boards.
Fool, as if you could take
the weather with you.

MOVING

Packing again: white suitcases
in the hall like a tiered wedding cake;
the curtains gone. Broad sun's brittle,
icing new shapes on the walls;
the cardboard boxes stacked
like bales of hay. Always burning
rules lines for fields that open
under smoke. Memory crops the past.
What we have harvested does not stay.
The old life will not, we say, be put down
on fresh pine, imagined flawless;
for some things cannot be laid.

Moving, we furnish new rooms
to be haunted with our love.
Rearranged the pictures raise
the ghosts upon the glass; the bills
arrive but are not paid; motes are bright
in a yellow sheaf, yet every grain
of light is loss. A morning's captured
honey glows, though beams of old-angled
blame still shine and play with spots of grief.

FOR EVER, AS IF

what keeps you going,
        old long player?
candour recorded
        fresh from the heart,
every note open
        & shining on
that spotless sleeve;
        the beat always
believed, & true

        from the body
you style us a
        way of singing,
 never locked
        in the groove – its
every move's
        felt fluency
spun straight from
        the wheel of black

though vinyl
        attracts the dust
what's compact
        lacks the long truth
of lyric persuasion –
        that nothing is
 ever a final blue: as if the
        music's playing,
seamless its soul, & forever
        that felt chord's
hurt is sound solace, as if
        there was no hiss
between the tracks for you

YEARBOOK

summer hides the text
in the sun-glanced
leaves: the surfaces
slide gold & cloud-
reflection tipped
with bird-shadow;
faint ripple-green,
& no sound; nothing
to detect in the slow
blue-burn of evening
across the lawn's
darkening page.
the air moves
& underleaf rises:
white flags to winter;
thin branches tangle:
keys pressed together;
fingers stray-fumble,
stuttering bird-marks
across a white sky;
the ink is smeared
by flight & the lie
of letters uneven.
in spring, clean words
fasten on the branches:
recounting afresh in
clawed feet, returning.

INDELIBLE

            The last bus
up to Wales, leaving
at four, this lovely
afternoon of late
summer, blue and
undercoat of gold.
The engine's early
winter cough is now
petrol-burred, running
past the pub where you
once drank: windows
boarded up these five
hard cold years; even
the sign's gone, along
with your old joke
made one smoky five-pint
night: you'd had to choose
between drinking and
driving and you chose
drinking.
            And next the
posts, which stand exactly
tall and do not grow,
announce a roll of seasons,
where each leaf's colour
is passed along in time
until the shape is dropped,
where every autumn
white marks out the cards
of green for play.
                Yet
there was another

field, which distance
will not wrap and send on
its way. September
mix of blue, and light's
Cotswold gold. A day
that though gone is yet
indelibly now. The first
boy is soft brown hair,
curving on the brow;
glasses with black frames
slightly too large. And
you remember how,
coming into work,
you heard: the mother,
her son and his friend
killed by a drunken
driver on their way
into school; and the
other: blond hair,
his ivory skin
that refused the sun;
day-dream rugby player
on the wing, the
line left without him,
his fingers plaited grass;
the ball's gone, God
knows where.
            But here's the foot-
hill, and soon the stop
where you alight, and
double language tells
this is the place of
priests, the clearing
that became the space
sacred to the saint

who's englished into
Andrew.
      It's evening,
and the last of blue's
flowing to red behind
the mountains. Memory
still cannot shed what
will not answer why
and tears but half reach
the eye, for loss kept
in the heart lives
but cannot cry.
          You placed white
flowers in a nest
of grief, the day they
planted *two thin trees to*
grow the tallest sky in
which small birds can rest.

BOYS ON THE TRAIN

blocked — that
means your mum
knows you're on it

no eye for fields
   skidding into
the past — & not
   one cow filed
in the memory

how good are you
at deleting your history?

yet this boy,
who says he will go
to the party dressed
as a rainbow,
is looking away
from his phone
& beyond the window,
where sun & rain build
an arch through which
he will never pass,
though his mind can
measure a radiant suit
— as if colour alone
could lead to treasure

FORME

The breaking of its pages marks the end for a book
and who knows what's beyond words fixed in a forme.
Letters stored are 'all sorts' needing a hand to declare
a view. To make meaning, count on what varies;
understand that types are movable, even when
the text coheres. Screw down the definitions and
remember how language, lying flat, must be pressed
in order to appear. Playing with verbs creates action
and existence; so then a series of ideas rises bright
as babies from new fonts: books so corvid-clever
you'd never think we would want for character
or plot, our clauses composed in crow-storms of ink.
Nearing the end-paper, yellow-skinned and foxed,
knowing nothing's left in the mould, each one of us
is a sole first edition. The glue's dry. Late years
prove what old binding lacks and plates fall out
as back and spine crack. The greatest fear cuts
an acid-burnt intaglio: what lies beyond gravure?
When all the words are broken will time survive?
If not, let's believe what we once thought and steal
back to the printers, to melt again and be re-set.

Forme: a body of type secured in a chase for printing

NOT FINDING

No registering how
the voice changes
from the inside

though finding it
is what you are
asked to do —

why say that
it's there, lying
essentially within:

words recovered
from the well of self,
a certain pitch?

If stone catches &
keeps half the voice
it throws back

the loss is here:
its emptiness the sound
absorbed by moss;

the pure flow
of first water's
singing underground:

a voice without
an echo &
never found:

no need to ask why
searching brings up
the bucket — dry.

THE HIDEAWAY SLEEP

TEL

all my phone calls are for Bradley Gardener

matt sky from the window
back white from the chemist

         & then these voices not for me
         Virgin, what have you done to my line?

rain writing & riddle
no sun to gloss the stone

         wrong, though I have got his number
         the question and sigh, always for him

failed development day
heart lost in the dark room

         he was never at this address
         the purity of what goes missing

six o'clock night calling
glow behind the curtain

         pick up echoes all this lost tone
         to answer is a shadow absence

unconnected weather
no star flash of old friend

         colder for his calls nothing knew
         the faceless chaste ignorance

elle is missing this now
we could have talked for hours

         few phrases unrehearsed
         my dead new address

Bradley Gardener, all my phone calls are for you

BROWN STUDIES

1

one tree grows
its bark covering
coffee-cream wood
until the axe shows
rings in the froth
frozen in the cup

2

the leather chair
is the colour of
the panelled room
or the earth-carpet
that does not move
under your feet
your thoughts are
of leaves thinning
or this hand-branch
breakdown of bone
fingering the scalp's
bald royal blue

the fallen ossuary
brittle brown floor
the loyalties of
tissue and cell
will not renew
this shred of bough
or foliage's coils

so little forest
to hide in or hold
you from the soil

3

bed's brown ship
aslant on an oak
floor patterned
like a wave about
to throw your
grainy dreams
against the wall

4

varnish accumulates
light on the surface
of the death box
till black gloves
extinguish the glint
on the handles &
raise you shoulder high
before the long drop in-
to the earth of the eyes
that sailed on the clouds

RAINFOREST, SHAME AND E-DELETE

Unabridged water-tongue
speaks in its flow: nothing wider
than the bank-breaker, dissolving
the anabranch – resisting definition
  of course
                in the forest
the man who knew the names,
treated fear, heart & fever, logs off:
cut down and fallen into river-space
  – the medicine hiding in the bark,
the seed's forgotten cure, the text
  of recovery astray in a leaf

    & what's in the mouth
changes colour, converted
 to eternal salt: the river sea,
dyeing in its own trumpet:
  an amazed zone of remedy
    lost in the Atlantic twist

A-WALKING RAIN

Home has shown
    a lasting roof
& lack of leaks
     proclaims repairs:
walls have dried
     wet charts of grief
& shutters are secure;
     the tiles are tight
in waves of slate
     that should not break
on shore; each pane
     is fast in wooden
frames – glass strong
      against the storm;
& bright in grates
      inside warm rooms
the fires assure.

    Yet clouds collect,
      from white-ocean
flowers, the floods
      that bloom again;
& though the house
      looks weather-proof
the wet has soaked
      the plaster; & there's one
slate that soon will crack
      to let in shafts of water;
hear the rain come walking,
a-walking down the stairs.

HIDEAWAY SLEEP

Fardel of nine to five born
by the fetch: the apparition
at work —
      falling off a chair
      at an interview, you
      gaze at the ceiling:
      rectangular but so
blessedly blank, a form
that you will not have to
fill in — through the long
      hours, you must keep
      the thought of the
      Hideaway Sleep,
platform of dream
in the topmost branches,
where leaf feeds on light:
      this is where
      the real self sits —
      a gathering of
      energy & song;
it is you raised up, as if far from
the facts on the ravening floor,
the figures & files;
      for now you must
      put these in that pile,
      those in this & speak of
      feud & office folderol;
at night, you'll come to the trunk
at the foot of the tree-house,
Hideaway Sleep,
      which to reach you
      must neither climb

nor creep; once you
could fly innocently;
now you must find a staircase
hidden in the shadows & ascend
without wings

BARON

even the ice monogrammed,
no doubt the flowers are fresh,
the shoes lacquered, breath moving
across the carpet: not a creak,
his boy answered the door;
the decanter catching the light
accurately chilled, just the faint
aftertaste of bargain varnishing
on the tongue, drying; besides, such
highly polished tables, warm wood
tints of older wines' tawny gloss –
perfectly pressed and the shirt
silk, of course; a small apartment
but traced with matchless shadows;
blue blazer with brass, and the wrist
fluid, waving as branches outside sway
hiding the leaf's palm, yet the watch's
expensive tick true, perhaps; his left
elbow resting on the velvet arm, the
tie-pin indubitably pale gold afternoon
glass covering the picture's patina blur
the frame's genuine, his words soft
and burnished syntax; yet the accent
hard to place, the black hair brushed
from the high forehead, his brown eyes
repainted again and again; his teeth wink
and go out; initials design to water.
morning will vanish the furniture.
no name to be found in the book

BOW-TIGHT

I

black-jail jacket:
only antidote to
the stiff white
ring hot-nailed
to the neck is the
bubble-wrapped
cells popping to
the sound of corkfire,
& later the triangle
in the top pocket
points down & there
is no stopping what
rushes the mouth
as the cold flush raises
white cuffs flapping
in a spattered bowl

II

a scratched cuff-link
lost at the dance is light
partying without you
& this silver star-struck
morning is dry; the
headache breaking,
the curtains open
& blind; though water
is remembering, cold
in hand, raised to the lips

MORNING FIGURE

shadow of boughs
on red brick
is a man running
towards a window:
long legs, left arm
stretched out, as
if to hail a taxi,
though his head
is only a twig
the breeze steers
a fingertip closer
to the ledge –
   will he leap &,
landing right on
the back seat of
the bed, wake
that man still
snoring on his
early morning
cloud – drive him
straight to where
the light shines
& that miracle
music plays all
night in the cave
of bright toys we
long to keep at
dawn?
      already
the wind stirs grey
leaf on the pillow –
warns of patterns

that repeat, shifting in
the dangerous day —
now here's a thin
white sheet crossing
the sun, & the branch
man fading into the
mortar —
       you'll not
see how he holds our
dreams together.

ANAESTHETISING THE AREA

How can you travel
         with an open wound, Heart,
& knowing all the days
         from which you will not recover?
So let us now stop
         the journey from reaching the capital:
arrest the movements
         in the burgeoning suburbs of love;
seal the avenue
         where the killings took place;
shut down the café
         in which the pain was served.
Let no one enter the square – for there the palace is built.

We will need more
         than ester, more than amide;
we will need real snow
         to cover the roofs of our dreams;
we will need frost & grains
         of oblivion to close the sex in the streets;
& give us that bright glacier,
         straight from the outhouse, to kill the topics of spring.

         & we will   want ice to
       narrow the   vein of yearning
     we will want   ice to lack the beating
      in the cage   & yes we will crave ice
       to be kept   in the red chambers of joy
     & the birds   to be frozen in the atria of hope

Let the only action be this action: the needle passing so slowly, yet so
accurately, through the flesh. It is a plea for the end of torment, a prayer for

the triumph of nothing; a song for a space that vanishes as the skin drifts over.

Yet, though the river is frozen
                            put your ear to its hard water:
hear how these old underground
                            griefs practise in a different sound.
Listen, there's something moving
                            fast below, like blood – and above, the first crack in the white

CUTTINGS

Remember

   Eye that looks on
filming is now;
  what was the world
is that first cut
that lies in snakes
 upon the floor;
  an old mind puts
 outtakes back a-
skew; what was will
   not renew.

Proleptic

 Boy, weeping for
lost damp nests, now
  smoking in stubb-
le, raw with fire,
the corn is cut
 every year;
   this is autumn's
  raze of light, which
shaves the swallows
   from the air.

HYPNAGOGIC

dreamer's sleep-laced eyes   see behind lids   an internal clime
cloudslip thought   space of early morning   the secret behind the word
lux tipping to knowledge   floating truth   warmth in the lenience of sheets
proof the trick in a dream   as reading the essence   drift to the edge
the real sun awakes   no blessing light of hand   the logos replaced
ceiling of glossed weather-shift   day's thin-truth laminate
shadow slight on the dial   gnomon, legerdemain & time

THE NIGHT VOICE

     – awaking with
the theme of sleep
   still sound, yet
knowing there is
   no way to keep
the score of what
   is found so deep
within – dream notes,
   night melodies –
for blood music
   will not transpose
to day, & chords'
   composed long rests
escape the stave –
   we rise & wipe
the record of
   arrangements

the city's beat
   deranges: horns,
sirens, alarms –
   & knowing what
we lack is that
   we listen for,
our sleeping tenor,
   we hope to catch it
through the clamour:
   frail as essential
birdsong, fading
   into traffic –

THE HOUSE OF SONG LOST IN THE CARPENTER'S TERMS

would work to form
from the forest

a house for the voice
built from complex grain

no note from the birdsmouth
the rafter won't sit correctly

this integrity of timbre
built with secret nailing

the invisible art pays
a price of hidden holes

no joiner's so wise
kerf – the gap made by a saw

yet cat's paw can't quite pull out
what's been struck in so deep

old story pole used to mark
the upward route to the stars

the stairs take us higher
where we found a hard landing

green long since seasoned
a crack splitting the heartwood

length of the hewn lilt
words shaped by the law's edge

last tunes lopped from the trunk
the history of sap filed as sawdust

STORM-CROSSED

— *storm hemmed with lightning*; black ghost of the hurricane
   that travelled the length of the fetch, powered by the warmth
of water: hews cliffs, tests chalk & sandstone: an old love's
   strength alive in the surge of an Atlantic bequest. Spirals
still double in the body, yet outside alone you know how
   wind fields cover the night: the harrowed cirrus conceals
star-bursts and the moon's halation. Passion never lost returns
   in the worst season, preserved by low pressure crossing as cloud
   when the heart's rhythm will fulminate, replayed as strike & rain.
   Memory of loss is still quick as wind falling: severance swifter
than speed in the eyewall: the heart of a tall tree broken: the blow,
   counter-clockwise, relights leaf each autumn, & blackening
branches restock the store of grief: birthright of the unrequited.
   Peace will be hoping for an age of hydrogen: your fair fortune
before death: flammable love kept amongst coolants, & nothing
   ignited; evening thoughts float, freethinking; soft forms
for water at leave in the weather: a shower, a spray in the breeze
   & at last the mind rising, lighter than elements, purer than air —

THE LACEMAKER LOOKING FOR A PATTERN

cordenette
    of cloud
      on blue ground
high trace of
      delicate hand
the wind raises
  lace from droplets
     the design
not repeated   each new
      pattern's printed
        on a different sheet

        ★

    rain falls straight
  gimp-heavy   threads
     couching low sky to field
    a bob of sun –
  the cross & twist
of light annealed on mud

   motifs as more than flow
the days' yield of connections
   are brides & bars –
  & at low tide
a causeway links isle to shore

        ★

the girl in the picture knows
there's no craft without looking
though hours are long against the blank wall
the painter praises
   the power of vision
       in light's fall

her night   voided patterning
the spaces left within black lace
   or stars as snowflakes
      stitching time to place...

THE WOODEN GODS

the wooden gods reign first –
hand-hewn, good stock,
still green with a forest spirit's
thirst for infinity
    Lighter
than rock, they open
& shut: Shentu & Yulei,
divinities of the door –
lock out the devils
conserve the pure
  or are
  a form of
  portable
  surety:
  half thin
  fine faces
  of forbears;
  half the
  carved
  heads of
  deities
  carried
  on a staff
tomorrow is the reign
of omnipresence,
which lacks form & weight;
no sense in borrowing
adze, saw & plane
or the concept of shape
to remake idols that never spoke:
Baal, Thoth & Lud, all grain dried out,
went up in smoke

        — in narrow streets,
where traders laugh by market stalls,
a dozen gods in a basket are sold
in a draughty hall, old lineaments still
alive in wood: charms revived as craft

SAWN & SHAPED

Stump

rings rearranged as a box –
six sides & a lock – to store
a dark block of light all square
the night is where you recall
the tree cut down on the hill
walk round a stump of dream
for roots remember water
rising to keep a forest green

Stub

breath turning to
cool blue curl
of smoke, white
collar above cork
crushed in glass:
a minute burning
in a line of ash

Shadow

a long stain on the world & at one with my movement in it
a following darkness not left behind in the sun though night
shows how what is here fades & presence is two shadows visiting

TARAXACUM TRISTE

I

moon-ticker

night, full-faced
  seedhead white

   malady of the
wind song matching
  sigh dispersal

   star feathery
clocks & the sickness:
  bald late love

   parachutes
deleted, lost in the
  unsoiled vasts

II

the roar

retreats:
old moon-
  mouth spits
  planets like
  teeth; *dent-
  de-lion,*
  lunacy
  of last
  grief: a
  a stalk
   left
    in the
     hand

QUEEN ANNE'S LACE

Carrot Plant

deeds of a herb —
  quiet specific;
a weed on
   the verge:
white invasion
 of a dry ditch;
  old usage
   urged by
 a witch
taught how
seeds (of carrot
plant) abort
  the embryo;
& her cunning
  keeps safe what
Soranus knew:
 a receipt, used
   in antiquity:
 bitterwort
mint, dittany
 — & rue

Natural Royal

within the umbrels
  little shade is
   a red centre
    where the
     wasps fly in;
      the lace's heart —

a drop of blood
pricked by the
Queen's own pin

YELLOW ARCHANGEL

    − at the world's ledge
  the toy clouds travel
     on blue May sky
in the bay the arc of the ship's yaw
     drawn by the current's drag

      staying &
   not leaping is the way to keep the eye
  fixed on home   foundations of fern
familiar bluebells past   & now a yellow archangel
lovelier dead nettle   brings the thought
  of looking closer   red honeyguides
   a flower with three green hearts
    the plant without
     a sting

APPOINTMENT

take good fear
for yourself
though they will
expert them-
selves clearly
be alert
your dentist's
twelve years old
& this vein
is tunnel-
ling out of
the body

please will you
complete this
norm though your
sexuality
is ticked here
as 'other'
this informed
nation will
help us to
record your
personal
free tales
in numbers

a weight comes
to those who
drink as if
good for you
red arches

on the whites
will show us
no smoke with-
out con-spire
in this world
of the vexed
o bees will
not make the
funny or
find above
this bullet
the point of
what we are
praying for
presume not
to think more
than units
per second
let them come
closer but
shoot when you
see the lights
of their wise —

THE HOUSE OF INHERITANCE

For Sarah Schosboek

My sister, who loves horses,
hates the sight of blood
and lay down on the deck
of a Seattle tram, faint after
reading the first chapter of
An Interview with a Vampire.

Across continents we swap
the texts of deep disease
conspiring in the bone;
each month awaits the maps
of similar afflictions: twin
contours are tumorous, forming
in the land beneath the skin.

Today she's on the phone:
Our Uncle Ray died of that!
What lives in her is a code
closer than anything next
to me: our dwelling together
in the house of inheritance.

Last night was a raid of shadows,
all riderless and teeming –
the hoofs thundering on the grass
till the stream faded sound
as blood absorbed the tracks.

Waking from dream as if one
early dawn was seeping into
separate rooms, we hear

the same new rain whispering
the last clue of the riddled body:
our flesh one wall on which
the damp shows through.

THE BLUE JUMPER

the blue jumper,
          blue — as the sky in a child's picture
with a cow in it
          — or the sea, painted
by a madwoman
          in the garden of an asylum
— or the eyes,
          indistinct indigo, looking down:
imago of the mother
          who bought and gave and wrapped
the blue jumper
          which was lost, years ago;
if left on a train
          where did it travel to?
if lent and unreturned
          did it keep the winters warm?
if draped like a wave
          over a chair in a seaside cafe
should we think of it
          as unclaimed, rewoven by spiders?
the picture that has
          a sky, blue as the blue jumper,
is not by a child
          though it has a great block of a cow in it;
yes, a white and brown
          udderless cow with a tail to tug for service;
under a red sun
          she grazes in a field of dismayingly yellow grass;
this does not matter
          as she has no mouth and no ears;
and she seems to live
          cheerfully with her disabilities,

as if remembering
            the old woman and the smell of her paint,
the shape of a madness
            that was, perhaps, some kind of recovery;
should you imagine yourself,
            painted into this picture, put in through compassion
or a desire for joy,
            it would be so much more ill-fitting,
even, than finding,
            loving and wearing the blue jumper,
as if you could be warm
            in the colour of her genius
when your head is
            swelling under the weave of the waves
and your fists are
            knuckle-twist in long sleeves of sea
as the tide pulls
            you down through its dark woollen mouth
and your thoughts
            are foam flying on a world of water.

NIGHT VISION

Lacking
a bright tapestry,
the tissue *tapedum*
lucidum, our night vision
  is one sixth of
    a cat's

  less than
  that of a spookfish
or dragonfly; we need
more to magnify the black
  sky & its width
    of stars.

  It was
  the war with darkness
that left radiance locked
in, waiting to be rescued
  by creation
    at work

  mining
  the world's brilliants
seamed for eternity.
Today's thermal, seeking warmth
    inside the
    enemy —

image
intensifies aim:
objects to be fired at
glow green; heat's the way to
sense & kill what's
unseen

though what
matters will be
asking how long rooms live
or suns sustain the spells of
colour in the
spectrum

our drive
is looking well for
guides on the dark flat road:
outside light is reflected
in the eyeshine of
the cat

REGARDING ROWANS

disks deplete
in the stream; what drove
the complete voice was born in the marrow:
cells forming to transport the joy of oxygen:
its risks of flesh & breath

a loss of
force in the telling
& sparrows' speech unsupported by songs
on the stave: autumn's anaemia is parsed
as parts of death & graves

veins narrow,
silted by roiling
flow, whilst the face is white, the count low; what
will transfuse is regarding rowans, blood-beaded
& thriving in poor soil

don't refuse
warm bright colour
in September that reminds of the lore
which ruled how what safeguards is stored in the twig
& planted at the door

remember
which winds stripped the stems
of all their leaves, for rich fruit will survive
on the relative of the rose: iron-red berries,
& strength before the fall

PRIVATE MEANS NOT SAYING

Stayed for twenty years
In the private suite
At the top of the Hotel.
A view of the weather:
The grey clouds tethered
To the peaks, the small
Stream that fed the lake.
A quiet man, and no trouble
    Till now, I said.

Spoke little, took breakfast
In bed, but dined every
Evening, alone at his table:
A book always open, a half
Bottle of red. You served
Him weekdays. A clever
Man, you'd heard it claimed:
Not famous but well read,
A scholar of private means,
An altogether silent man,
    Is what you said.

Not a friend the whole time
He was staying; some hours
By himself at the bar, a drop
Too much, but never – no –
Not drunk, as such. Always
Courteous and well bred. He
Walked among the princes
Of the past, and every date
Was in his head. His only
Ladies lived and loved

In yellowed pages his fingers
     Turned, she said.

Taught at the grey school
That stands towered at the head
Of the valley, where the wind
Choirs through many doors.
Unwed, he bound his knot
To history, and took his game
On sodden fields each Thursday.
It's said he did not take a wage
But gave the salt of knowledge.
Unsalaried, he kept apart and
Spent breaks entombed with
Leather on the shelf. We should
Not state he had no heart: he
Loved the past instead. Keeping
To his own wealth, he did not
Grace our Common Room,
But with himself, dry-tongued,
Lived as if waiting for
     Silence, we said.

He took the pink one every
Day, but never spoke of money.
You'd think he knew just when
To play and where the markets
Led: the sun-wink on his shoes
Showed he'd quit while still
Ahead. One month when
Buried deep in a different
Era, he bought not sold;
The line, mislead, moved
Lower. Yet still he'd trade
By fire and storm; he'd blaze

As winds blew harder and with
A mind of Drake disperse the bears
And their Armada. He never
Used a stop; would only buy
Or hold. But when Black Monday
Turned the screens to red,
He had no fleets of gold.
Too late to sell: a paper loss
Became the death of credit.
What was never realized could
Not be changed to bread. This was
      My life, you said.

He is dispersed pronominally.
I heard he cut a graph, knife-
Jagged in his wrist; you claimed
He'd used a bed of bath, the very
Hottest, or so we said;
He'd had no wife, son or
Daughter; it's true he did
Not lock the door, the night
They found him dead; she
Saw the tiles marked with hands,
The places where he'd bled:
The lines of gore, going long
And dripping down, went
Right across his head. And
When at last you pulled the
Plug, there formed a rose of
Water, a bloom of white and
Red. Pray what flows as one
Will reunite,
            They said.

ANTI-PASTORAL

– path through tall hedges,
a pot-holed track of earth
and rock that must once have
been gravelled; landslip of
small stones, sand, swept away
o how long ago; all
leads down to the floodplains,
now dry in hot summer,
the fields baked to a jig-
saw of cracked mud, even
the dark ditch's deep wounds
scab at the edges, tuft
with thin cotton grass, frail
as the last fibres that
linger, light on the flesh,
after the bandage has
risen with the mist, re-
moved to the high blue day.
    In the distance, two
bridges, delicate
as if painted on a
Japanese screen
draw a man into
the landscape, where it
is as if he knows
the path and the scree,
the stones that are a script,
an even darker grey
than the paper on which
the slow spell is written that
charms him across the
bridge until he can see

the woods where he knows
a great grey house is hidden
with its secrets: priest-
holes and old silver, glint-
bright behind panelling
waxed with timelight, and, as
ancient as the wide park,
the tall screen of the trees
tarpaulins the grey-skinned
tower blocks in summer –
leaf to soak up autoscreech,
the scream and dazzle of
bladefight – whispers where
grass-song softens the
rustle of notes exchanged
in alleys and stairwells,
the knife-hiss in the streets.
   So he imagines,
for a moment, how the
poem-park elegance once
had an eighteenth-
century air, a frieze
of cold cattle po-
sitioned to denote
ownership of lush
grass – unlike the dry
colour of the trees,
lemony – though patched
with evergreen, as if
the assonance of what
was could live at ease with
what he now sees
in the lengths of afternoon light:
the burnt-out car, windows
glassless and metal scorched

black-blue like the bruises
above the flame-licked white
steel cheeks of the children
who drove the car from the city
where the measure of the street
broke the feet, which once
tripped in the park, and the vis-
tas were endstopped by
conifers and the dance
reeled into the rusting
brook with spinning wheels,
the midnight melted tyres;
yet the syllables survive
the anti-grammar in
the eyes that reflected
the flames that will not burn
the walk of a man who
steps with one pace out of —

NOT BY ME

This poem was not written by me.
Should I send it packing, with its suitcases of shrill similes.
Its sly attempts at humour; its lines that do not scan.
Its hero with no story; its half-rhymes that clang.
I'll wave it on its way: its dead metaphors stink.

This poem was not written by, I think.
Should I watch its fat stanzas waddle away
Or store a few images for another day,
And put line nine that's bright like a bang
In the left luggage locker or a security van.

But this poem was not written by me.
My work stopped rhyming in nineteen eighty-three.
There's a dead sheep in line thirteen.
It could be a symbol, but where has it been?
It could have been rural or belonged to God,

And I'd like to get rid of it but that's proving hard
Because this poem does not belong to me.
Its rhythms are irregular. I should show it the door
Or at least put it away in the bottom drawer,
And wait until it stinks.

I hope that no one thinks that the last line was too short
And that I have no control over my craft
Because this poem was not written by me.
It's just stopped rhyming; it hasn't got my voice.
Yet it still keeps coming. I haven't got a choice.

Every time the verse tries to wriggle free
There's a metre thumping that's not to do with me.

I'll open the sad suitcase, and let the rhymes fall out
I'll let its words wither, for there is no doubt
This poem was not written by me.

These words that spin across the page
Seem to have come from a different age
Where the rhymes pop one by one
And the rhythm kicks like the dead and gone.
The beat is the beat of rigor mortis

And now my only thought is –
That this poem does not belong to me.
That it's still being written is a tragedy.
Its words are emerging from a pale mist.
It hasn't got a plot; it has no twist,

But every time I try to bring it to an end
It just keeps going with its blend
Of five-line stanzas and a way with metaphor
That's highly ineffective or been used before.
Yes, there is no doubt that it's been a flop.

I don't know where it comes from but really it must stop.
So I won't dally; this stanza is a crime,
Though there is the bonanza of three extra lines
And one fairly good example of internal rhyme.
I don't want the credit for I know without a doubt
(And I don't want to threaten, I don't want to shout,
So I'll just say this quietly, and then let you be):
This poem, yes this poem, is not by me.

THANKS

My thanks go to the following: Alex Wylie, for his help in editing this book; Todd Swift, for publishing it; and members of Border Poets, for their comments on some of the poems included here. The errors are mine alone.

ACKNOWLEDGEMENTS

Some of the poems in this collection have either
appeared or are forthcoming in the following magazines
and anthologies:

THE GLAZIER'S CHOICE

491 Magazine – Maryland, USA ('Vacant Possession',
'Yearbook'), *Aesthetica Creative Writing Annual; Assent*
('The Clearance'); ('Order'); *Bare Fiction* ('Twitch');
Crannog – Eire ('Moving', 'Half Heraclitean');
Envoi ('Void Post'); *Fire* ('Boarding the Dark', 'The
Storyteller'); *Magma* ('The Defective Lens'); *MiPOEsias*
– Florida, USA ('For ever, as If'); *New Writer*
('Jackdaws'); *Other Poetry* (Looking In', 'No Longer
the Only'); *Pennine Platform* ('The Humour Tree');
Poetry Salzburg – Austria ('Indelible', 'Private Means
Not Saying', 'Rule', 'To Be In Touch', 'The Glazier's
Choice'); *Prick of the Spindle* – Louisiana, USA ('The
Train Library', 'Evening Macon Gold'); *Prime Number* –
North Carolina, USA ('Not Finding') ; *Prole* ('Change
of Use'); *Raintown Review* – Maryland, USA ('Six
Months'); *San Pedro River Review* – California, USA
('The True Sun'); *Scintilla* ('Hidden', 'Forme'); *The Echo
Room* ('The Teacher's Clothes Dyed In-service', 'Flight
Escape'); *The Interpreter's House* ('To My Successor',
'Boys on the Train'); *The Reader* ('Double Vision'); *The
SHOp* – Republic of Ireland ('The Garden', 'The Irish
Semiologist Advises the Poet', 'The Words Moving
Away'), *The Warwick Review* ('Water Laughing'); *Under
the Radar* ('Leaving', 'View').

and/or – New York State, USA ('Baron'); *Bellow Literary Review* – Louisiana, USA ('Bow-tight'); *Earthlines* ('Rainforest, shame & e-delete'); *Envoi* ('Regarding Rowans'); *The Iron Book of Humorous Verse*, Iron Press ('Not By Me'); *New Walk* ('Brown Studies', 'Storm-crossed'); *Orbis* – ('Tel'); *Petrichor Machine* – New Hampshire, USA ('Morning Figure'); *Poetry Salzburg* – Austria ('Anti-pastoral', 'Appointment', 'Cuttings', 'Hypnagogic', 'Sawn & Shaped', 'Private Means Not Saying'); *Skidrow Penthouse* – New York, USA ('The Night Voice'); *Tears in the Fence* ('The House of Song Lost in the Carpenter's Terms', 'Queen Anne's Lace', 'The Lacemaker Looking for a Pattern', 'The Wooden Gods'); *The Conium Review* – Oregon, USA ('The Hideaway Sleep'); *Third Wednesday* – Michigan, USA and *The Nettle Trick Anthology* ('The Blue Jumper'); *The Madison Review* – Wisconsin, USA ('The House of Inheritance'); *The New Writer* ('A-Walking Rain'); *The Poetry Bus* – Republic of Ireland ('Anaesthetising the Area' – nominated for a Pushcart Prize); *Under the Radar* ('Yellow Archangel', 'Night Vision').

'Taraxacum Triste' appeared in the online journal *BlazeVox*.